Sharper Thinking
from Kids to Adults

Tom Stohlgren

1

Dedication

This booklet is dedicated to Jim Stohlgren, Dave Parsons, David Graber, Steve DeBenedetti, Jim Quinn, Dan Binkley, Jim and Linda Detling, Carl Sagan, Madalyn Murray O'Haire, Richard Dawkins, Lewis Vaughn, Theodore Schick, Neil deGrasse Tyson, George Carlin, Bill Maher, David Fischer, Cindy Osterman-Stohlgren, John Giuntoli, my children, and over one hundred other "scientists, teachers, philosophers, and confidants" who have influenced my thinking over the years.

My Favorite Inspirational Quote:
"[It's] not important to get children to read. Children who wanna read are gonna read. Kids who want to learn to read are going to learn to read. [It's] much more important to teach children to question what they read. Children should be taught to question everything. To question everything they read, everything they hear." -- George Carlin (March, 2008)

Table of Contents

Introduction

I taught university classes in "Critical Thinking" for over a decade at a major university before realizing that we should be reaching a younger and broader age group of students. These skills are important for ages 9 to 99, much like Aesop's fables, which were told 2,500 years ago for adults and covered religious, social, and political themes. From the Renaissance onward, they were used as ethical guides to educate children.

If I were explaining what sharper thinking is to a pre-teen or teen, I would purposely select a simpler vocabulary and tailor my discussion to match their life experiences to date. I would begin by saying that sharper thinking is being a good problem solver, something like being a detective. You're seeking evidence to support a claim made by a friend, a teacher, a pastor, and even a parent. It's about not automatically accepting everything you hear or see but thinking carefully and asking smart questions to figure out what makes sense.

When you use sharper thinking, you:

- Look at all the information you have.
- Ask questions like, "Is this true? How do I know?"
- Think about different sides of the situation.
- Decide what makes the most sense based on facts, not just opinions.

Sharper thinking helps you make good decisions, solve problems, and understand the world better!

If I were explaining sharper thinking to an adult, I would note that sharper thinking is the process of actively and skillfully analyzing, evaluating, and synthesizing information to make reasoned decisions or solve problems. It involves questioning assumptions, identifying biases, assessing evidence, and considering multiple perspectives to arrive at a well-founded conclusion. The key aspects of sharper thinking for adults include:

- **Curiosity:** Asking "why," "how," and "what if" questions to deepen understanding.

- **Analysis:** Breaking information into parts to understand it better.
- **Evaluation:** Judging the reliability of sources and the strength of evidence.
- **Logic:** Connecting ideas in a way that makes sense and avoids contradictions.
- **Reflection:** Considering the implications of a decision or viewpoint and revisiting it if necessary. Does new evidence continue to support your conclusions?

For example, when reading a news article, a sharper thinker might ask:

- "Who wrote this, and what might their perspective or bias be?"
- "What evidence supports the claims made here?"
- "Are there other viewpoints or additional information that I should consider?"

By practicing sharper thinking, everyone from pre-teens to elderly adults can navigate complex information, avoid manipulation, and make informed, thoughtful choices.

Albert Schweitzer said, "Example is the best teacher." Examples often help in describing complex issues.

Teaching sharper thinking skills to such a broad audience range might be taught the same way. The messaging can be clear to young and old if taught in a simple and fun way with talking animals. I've included a trickster Coyote, a gullible Squirrel, a skeptical Mouse, and a Wise Old Owl to illustrate sharper thinking skills. The game is to expose the thinking mistakes of the trickster Coyote, avoid being as gullible as the Squirrel, learn to be skeptical like the Mouse, and appreciate the thinking mastery of the Wise Old Owl.

I like to think I'm a wise old owl, but I sometimes make mistakes, too. Maybe everyone is part Coyote, Squirrel, Mouse, and Wise Old Owl, but our goal is to learn to think more like Wise Old Owls all the time.

No matter if it's a trickster Coyote, the gullible Squirrel, or the skeptical Mouse speaking to you, you must try to use the Owl's reasoning to ask questions, look at the evidence, and figure out whether what they are telling you makes sense.

Becoming a Wise Old Owl in conversations isn't easy, especially with someone who makes mistakes in their thinking. A "fallacy" is like a trick or a mistake usually made in the Coyote's thinking. Young people make a lot of mistakes, but so do a surprising number of adults in daily conversations. Sharper thinking helps you spot the tricks and mistakes in everyday conversations.

There are many reasons Coyotes make mistakes and why some Squirrels and Mice believe them:
- **It's easier:** Coyotes are often quick thinkers. It's quicker to believe something without checking if it's true. Checking facts takes time and effort. Many Coyotes don't take the time to check themselves, so a Wise Old Owl must do it for them.
- **It's emotional:** Some Coyotes are filled with strong emotions or aggression. Squirrels and Mice might be easily pushed around.

- **We hear it often:** If every Coyote and Squirrel around you says something, you might start believing it, even if it's not true.
- **It's what everyone wants to believe:** Sometimes, we believe things because it makes us feel better or because they fit in with what we already think.

Sharper thinking helps us stop and think, "Is this true?" instead of blindly believing the first thing we hear. But fallacies can be tricky, so it takes practice to spot them! I wrote this short booklet to help young people and adults spot them.

In the stories that follow, I'll give examples of common fallacies and teach you how to spot them and avoid them, no matter if the person using the fallacy is your best friend, classmate, family member, neighbor, salesperson, advertiser, doctor, lawyer, teacher, or even your favorite pastor or parent. Everyone uses fallacies occasionally, so be prepared.

Fallacies

The Personal Attack Fallacy

The hungry, old Coyote went into a forest to hunt rabbits when he came across the Squirrel sitting safely above him in a tree.

'I'm looking for rabbits tonight,' Coyote said.

'You may be looking in the wrong place,' the Squirrel replied, 'Rabbits prefer grasslands and shrublands.'

The Coyote glared at the Squirrel. 'Why should I believe you? You are the ugliest Squirrel I have ever seen.'

The Coyote licked his chops and walked on.

The Coyote came to a cliff with a Mouse safely sitting atop it.

'I'm looking for rabbits tonight,' Coyote said.

You may be looking in the wrong place,' the Mouse replied, 'Rabbits prefer grasslands and shrublands.'

The Coyote glared at the Mouse. 'Why should I believe you? You are the smallest Mouse I have ever seen.'

The Coyote licked his chops and walked on.

The Coyote came to an oak tree with a Wise Old Owl perched safely on a branch.

'I'm looking for rabbits tonight,' Coyote said.

'You may be looking in the wrong place,' the Wise Old Owl replied, 'Rabbits prefer grasslands and shrublands.'

The Coyote glared at the Owl, but the Wise Old Owl glared back.

The Wise Old Owl scolded the Coyote. 'Why should any animal provide you truthful information when you personally attack animals that try to help you?'

Discussion Question: Why did the Coyote go hungry that night?

Explanation: The personal attack (or ad hominem) fallacy happens when, instead of talking about someone's idea or opinion, they attack the person. This is sometimes called a character assassination and can range from simple name-calling to slander. It's like saying something mean about someone to try to prove them wrong instead of discussing the actual topic.

The Red Herring Fallacy

The old Coyote was known far and wide as an expert thief who always avoided getting caught.

One day, the old Coyote stole a banana from Squirrel's house and an apple from Mouse's house. Coyote fur was found at each house.

When the Squirrel and Mouse reported the thefts to the Wise Old Owl, the Owl sent the Squirrel and Mouse to question the thief while the Wise Old Owl called the police.

The Coyote was in a particularly nasty and defensive mood when he was confronted by the Squirrel. 'Did you steal the banana from my house?' Squirrel bravely asked the Coyote.

'Why would anyone steal a banana instead of an apple?' Coyote asked. 'Apples are lower in levels of carbohydrates and total sugars.'

The gullible Squirrel thought for a moment and then nodded 'yes.' 'What you say is true, Coyote. I never thought of it that way.'

Just then, the skeptical Mouse scampered up to confront the old Coyote.

'Did you steal the apple from my house?' the Mouse bravely asked the old Coyote.

'Why would anyone steal an apple instead of a banana?' the old Coyote yelled. 'Bananas have higher levels of vitamins.'

The skeptical Mouse paused to think about the old Coyote's answer.

'The vitamins are not important here,' Mouse said. 'Squirrel and I want to know if you stole our fruit.'

Just then, the Wise Old Owl swooped down from atop a nearby tree and blocked the old Coyote's escape with his sharp talons and beak. A police siren howled in the distance.

Wise Old Owl patted the Mouse on the back and glared at the old Coyote.

The Owl continued, 'All your talk about vitamins and calories was meant to distract us from answering the most important question: Did you or did you not steal the fruit from their houses? Your evasive answers were red herrings. We found your fur at the scenes of the crime.'

The old Coyote looked at the police officer with paw-cuffs stomping toward them.

'I want to see my lawyer,' the old Coyote said.

Discussion Question: Did the old Coyote's red herrings work?

Explanation: The red herring fallacy happens when someone tries to distract you from the main topic by bringing up something else that isn't related. It's like if you ask about one thing, but the person changes the subject, so you stop thinking about the real question.

The False Choice (or False Dichotomy) Fallacy

The old Coyote was being his typically bossy self when he cornered the gullible Squirrel on a street corner.

'Listen, Squirrel, you can either come to the park and play baseball with everyone or stay home and be bored all day!' Coyote said.

The Squirrel responded in a wimpy tone and said, 'I don't want to be bored all day, that's for sure. Let's see if Mouse wants to play baseball at the park.' They walked on until they found the skeptical Mouse eating seeds and enjoying the sunshine.

'Listen, Mouse, you can either come to the park and play baseball with everyone or stay home and be bored all day!' Coyote said.

'Baseball doesn't sound so bad,' Squirrel said.

The skeptical Mouse became agitated. He blinked his eyes and wiggled his ears as he thought. 'Why are there only two options on what to do on a beautiful day?' the Mouse asked the Coyote.

The Wise Old Owl swooped down from a tree, patted the Mouse on the back, smirked at the Squirrel, and glared at the old Coyote.

'You are correct, Mouse,' said the Wise Old Owl. 'There are many ways to spend a beautiful day, such as reading a good book, taking a nature hike, or playing on a playground.'

Discussion Question: What do you think the old Coyote tried to accomplish?

Explanation: A false choice (or false dichotomy) is when someone says there are only two choices when there could be more options. It's like saying, "You have to pick one or the other," even though there might be other possibilities.

The Hasty Generalization Fallacy

The old Coyote stood on the stairs of the Town Hall to complain to everyone in town. 'Everyone without a real, paying job should be driven from town!' the Coyote said. 'I met one today and he was begging for money. They are all a blight on our town.'

The gullible Squirrel looked around and did not see anyone begging, but Squirrel nodded in general agreement.

The skeptical Mouse overheard the Coyote and immediately rolled her eyes and shook her head, 'No.' 'My aunt is a retired doctor, my dad is a stay-at-home dad, and my baby sister is too young to work.'

The Wise Old Owl swooped down from a tree, patted the Mouse on the back, smirked at the Squirrel, and glared at the old Coyote.

19

'The Mouse thought about what you said, Coyote. Many people without paying jobs contribute dearly to families and the community. You based your conclusion on too little information.'

'Maybe I did,' the old Coyote said. 'I should have looked for one more beggar.'

Discussion Question: Would finding one more beggar justify the Coyote's plan?

Explanation: A hasty generalization is when someone makes a big statement about something based on too little information. It's like deciding too quickly without knowing enough to be fair.

The Strawman Fallacy

The Coyote, Squirrel, and Mouse were walking down the road having a polite conversation when the Mouse spoke up about something that was troubling her.

'My parents said I should not listen to you, Coyote,' Mouse said.

'My parents think you're a bad influence, Coyote,' Squirrel said.

'Maybe both your parents don't want you to listen to any other animals,' the Coyote said. 'They only want you to listen to them! Your big bosses!'

'That's the dumbest idea I ever heard,' the Mouse said. 'That's not what they're talking about. They were talking about you, Coyote!'

The Wise Old Owl swooped down from a tree, patted the Mouse and the Squirrel on the back, and glared at the old Coyote as he snuck away.

'Right,' said the Wise Old Owl. 'The old Coyote offered up a strawman plan that would prevent you from listening to anyone but your parents, including teachers and trusted community members and friends. It's important to listen to different and trusted sources while avoiding bad influences.'

Discussion Question: What reasons might people have to offer a strawman's plan?

Explanation: The strawman fallacy happens when someone exaggerates what another person said to make it sound silly or easier to argue against. It's like setting up a pretend version of what the person said and then arguing against that, instead of what they actually said.

The Slippery Slope Fallacy

The Coyote, Squirrel, and Mouse strolled through a park one day when the Squirrel became overcome with hunger.

'Coyote, you have walked all over this park, and indeed, all over this forest and county. My little legs are too small to survey such a large area. Where might a starving Squirrel like me find a tree around here with a stash of delicious acorns?'

The Mouse sympathized with the Squirrel. 'Yes, Coyote, surely with your vast knowledge of the park, you could guide my friend Squirrel to a productive oak tree in the area.'

'It would do you no harm,' Squirrel added sheepishly.

The Coyote laughed in a teasing, cruel manner. 'I couldn't, in all good conscience, point you to a food stash. Once I did that, you'd want me to draw you a map of all the productive oak trees in the whole park. After that, you'd have me map all of the productive oak trees in the forest, and after that, in the whole county.

The Squirrel began to moan in hunger.

The Wise Old Owl swooped down from a tree, patted the Mouse on the back, hugged the Squirrel, and glared at the old Coyote.

'The Coyote is being unnecessarily cruel, Squirrel,' the Owl said. 'He knew there was a big acorn tree just up ahead. He had no reason to believe you would ask him to map all the trees in the county! There was no such slippery slope!'

The old Coyote snuck away.

Discussion Question: Why is the use of a slippery slope in conversation effective?

Explanation: The slippery slope fallacy is when someone thinks that if one thing happens, it will start a chain of events that leads to something extreme or bad—even though there's no good reason to believe all those steps will actually happen.

The Appeal to Ignorance Fallacy

The old Coyote, gullible Squirrel, and skeptical Mouse were hiking in a deep, dark forest one day when they all heard the crackling of branches in the distance.

The old Coyote shook in fear and looked around suspiciously. This was an unusual sight for the Squirrel and Mouse to see.

'What's the matter, Coyote?' Mouse asked.

'I've never seen you look scared,' said the Squirrel.

'It's Bigfoot, I'm sure!' said Coyote.

Squirrel looks around in fright. 'Bigfoot? The nine-foot-tall ape-like monster that hunters are looking for on all those TV shows? It could be!'

The Mouse shakes her head in disgust. 'All those shows where they never quite find Bigfoot?'

The old Coyote gets furious at Mouse. 'That doesn't prove it doesn't exist!'

The Wise Old Owl swoops down from a tree, pats the Mouse on the back, hugs the Squirrel, and glares at the old Coyote.

'On this rare occasion, Coyote is correct,' Owl said. 'However, not having proof doesn't make it true; it just means we don't know for sure. And, if you ask me, I'd say it's silly to be frightened of things that may not exist, like ghosts, fire-breathing dragons, aliens from outer space...

The Wise Old Owl's voice tapers off as he continued to provide examples of things that may not exist.

'... the Loch Ness Monster, witches, Darth Vader, Godzilla, zombies...'

Discussion Question: Can you name other monsters featured on TV and in movies that may not exist in real life? [Hint: the Wise Old Owl's list is endless.]

Explanation: The appeal to ignorance fallacy happens when someone says something must be true (or false) just because there's no proof either way. It's like saying, 'Since we don't know for sure, it has to be the way I think.' But just because there's no proof doesn't mean something is automatically true or false!

The False Analogy Fallacy

When the old Coyote saw Squirrel and Mouse on their way to school, he quickly pounced in front of them. 'Where do you think you're going?' asked Coyote in a harsh voice.

'School,' replied the Squirrel and Mouse at the same time.

'School is just like jail,' laughed Coyote. 'School and jail are exactly the same. They both have a long list of rules to follow and you can't leave whenever you want.'

'That's kind of true,' said gullible Squirrel. 'I never thought of it that way.'

"That's why I quit going to school," said Coyote. 'And look at me now!'

The skeptical Mouse rolls her eyes and wiggles her ears as she thinks. 'I don't think they are exactly alike,' Mouse said to the Coyote. 'Schools teach us many good things, and jail is a punishment for doing bad things.'

The Wise Old Owl swoops down from a tree, pats the Mouse on the back, hugs the Squirrel, and glares at the old Coyote.

'The Mouse is right again,' the Wise Old Owl said. 'The Coyote focused only on two things school and jail had in common. His comparison is incomplete and misleading. I'm guessing that there aren't too many people in jail who didn't wish they were in a school instead.'

The Coyote sneaks away.

Discussion Question: What makes a false analogy easy to detect when someone is trying to trick you?

Explanation: A false analogy is when someone compares two things that aren't really similar, and then uses that comparison to argue something. It's like saying two things are the same just because they have a few things in common, even though they might be very different in important ways.

The Begging the Question Fallacy

The old Coyote stood outside a college campus waving a blank sheet of paper. 'It is well known that I am a wily Coyote because I am the smartest Coyote that ever lived.'

The Squirrel looked on in amazement while the Mouse looked on suspiciously.

'I knew he was smart, but even I didn't know he was the smartest Coyote that ever lived,' the Squirrel said.

'That's right,' Coyote said. 'The smartest Coyote that ever lived. That proves I'm smart.'

The skeptical mouse rolls her eyes and wiggles her ears as she thinks. 'It looks like Coyote is waving a blank piece of paper," Mouse whispered to the Squirrel.

That shows he doesn't need a college diploma to prove he's so smart,' Squirrel said.

'But he's offered no proof that he's smart,' Mouse said.

The Wise Old Owl swoops down from a tree, pats the Mouse on the back, shakes her head in disgust, and glares at the old Coyote.

'No proof, indeed,' the Wise Old Owl said. 'Coyote repeats himself so often that others are less likely to demand proof that what he says is true. That's begging the question.'

Discussion Question: Why do you think many animals repeat themselves so many times?

Explanation: Begging the question happens when someone tries to prove something by just repeating it differently, without giving any real proof or explanation. It's like saying something is true just because you said it is, without showing why.

The Causal Fallacy

The Coyote, Squirrel, and Mouse strolled through the park on a night with a full moon.

'Ah, a full moon!' Coyote said. 'It's a well-known fact that all animals act crazier on nights with a full moon!'

'Now that you mention it, Coyote, I think we certainly do,' Squirrel said.

The skeptical mouse rolls her eyes in disgust. Mouse whispered to the Squirrel. 'Maybe you can see more animals when the moon is full.'

'That wouldn't explain a greater number of them acting crazier,' Coyote said.

'What if more animals are acting crazier on darker nights, but you can't see them as well?' Mouse asked the Coyote.

34

The Wise Old Owl swoops down from a tree, pats the Mouse on the back, shakes her head in disgust at the Squirrel, and glares at the old Coyote.

'No proof, once again, Coyote' the Wise Old Owl said. 'You have not shown that the full moon causes animals to be crazier, only that you might be able to see them better. There is no real connection between the phase of the moon and crazier animal behavior.'

Discussion Question: How do you think a cloudy night would affect animal behavior on the night of a full moon?

Explanation: A causal fallacy happens when someone thinks one thing causes another thing to happen. But just because something happens at the same time doesn't mean one thing caused the other. It's important to check if things really are connected before deciding that one caused the other.

The Appeal to Authority Fallacy

The ambitious Coyote was recruiting animals for his "Unicorn Club" when he came upon the gullible Squirrel. 'You must join my Unicorn Club, Squirrel,' he said. 'The only requirement is that you believe that unicorns are real.'

'How do we know that unicorns truly exist?' asked Squirrel.

'That's the easy part,' said Coyote. 'Unicorns were written about over two thousand years ago by Ctesias, a famous Greek historian and doctor.'

'Wow,' said Squirrel. 'A historian and a doctor!'

Coyote continued, 'Unicorns were well known to the ancient people of India, Persia, and Greece and featured in art and books. Someone as famous as Ctesias can't be wrong!' 36

'You are probably right,' Squirrel said, 'and I had better tell my friend, Mouse, about your club.'

The Coyote and Squirrel walked on to find Mouse eating seeds in a field.

'Mouse,' they said, 'You must join the Unicorn Club.'

'I've never seen a unicorn,' Mouse replied. 'I should ask the Wise Old Owl.'

'Ctesias has never been wrong!' Coyote said. 'And almost everyone believes that unicorns are real, and you don't want to be left out of the Unicorn Club.'

The Mouse walked on to find the Wise Old Owl and told him about the Coyote and Squirrel.

'Ctesias and the ancient Greeks believed many things we don't believe today,' Owl said. 'Wait until you see and pet a unicorn before you believe in them.'

Discussion Question: What do you think about Owl's advice?

Explanation: The appeal to authority fallacy happens when someone says something is true just because an important or famous person says so, instead of giving good reasons or facts to show it's true. An evidence-based learner needs supporting facts to justify a claim.

Evidence-based Learning: The Scientific Method

Owl Teaches the Scientific Method

The Wise Old Owl offered a free class in the scientific method and to help the Coyote, Squirrel, and Mouse become evidence-based learners. They all showed up for the class.

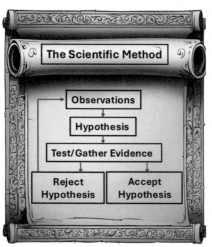

Owl began by saying, 'The Scientific Method is a guide for answering questions about the world around us with evidence rather than someone's untested beliefs.'

'It teaches you <u>how</u> to think, not <u>what</u> to think. It begins with your curiosity, observations, and questions,' Owl continued.

40

Coyote became angry. 'I'll believe what I want to believe,' he said. 'I'm leaving! Squirrel, if you know what's good for you, you'll leave too!'

The Coyote stormed out of the class.

Squirrel looked confused by the Coyote's decision, so the Mouse reassured him.

'There's no harm in listening to what the Wise Old Owl has to say,' Mouse said.

The Squirrel stayed and listened, but he was easily distracted during the entire lesson.

'What kind of oak trees make the best acorns for squirrels -- white oaks or red oaks?' Owl asked Squirrel.

Squirrel was suddenly interested.

'I don't know,' Squirrel said.

'Make a guess,' said Owl.

Squirrel said, 'I would guess the red oaks because I like the looks of those trees.'

'Let's do some research,' Mouse said.

Owl smiled as the Squirrel and Mouse walked through the park observing other squirrels, collecting acorns, and tasting them for good measure.

After a long day, they returned to Owl's classroom.

'How many squirrels did you see eating red oak acorns and white oak acorns?' Owl asked.

'We saw 49 squirrels eating white oak acorns, but only 17 eating red oak acorns,' Mouse said.

'I know why,' Squirrel said. He tasted a red oak acorn and spit it out. 'These taste bitter!'

'They are higher in chemicals called tannins, making them bitter,' Owl said.

'White oak acorns win,' said Mouse.

'Squirrel wins too,' the Owl said. 'He knows where to shop for food!'

They all laughed.

'That's science,' Owl said. 'You asked a question, made a guess, gathered evidence, and learned something new. That's evidence-based learning.'

Discussion Questions:
What do you think would happen if they repeated that experiment at a different park?
Do you think other squirrels might benefit from those research results?
What do you think the Coyote would say if he watched the Mouse and Squirrel conduct their experiment?

Supporting Information: See Additional Resources (Page 59).

Examples of Sharper Thinking

Pretenders in Science:
Is the Earth Flat?

The old Coyote stood on the college steps waving a carpenter's level and yelling at students passing by.

'The Earth is flat, I'm telling you,' Coyote said. 'For thousands of years, we've known the Earth is flat and I now can prove it with a simple carpenter's level!'

The gullible Squirrel and skeptical Mouse wandered by to listen to the Coyote. They saw his carpenter's level on the ground.

'He's right,' Squirrel said. 'Many thought the world was flat for a long time.'

Coyote continued, 'That's right, Squirrel! And no matter where you travel, you can take out your carpenter's level, place it on the ground, and you will see evidence that the Earth is flat!"

The Coyote places his carpenter's level on another spot on the ground, and it "reads" level.

'It does read level,' Squirrel says. 'The Earth seems to be flat."

The Mouse rolls her eyes and wiggles her ears in thought.

'That's the scientific method for you,' Coyote laughed. 'I believed it before I even started my experiment. I made my guess that it was flat, and the carpenter's level proves it beyond the shadow of a doubt! If I take a plane trip anywhere on Earth, step off the plane, and take a similar reading, my guess is it will also be level,' the Coyote said.

'That may be because airports are built in flat areas,' said Mouse as she studied the shape, size, and location of the bubble inside the carpenter's level.

'The shape of the bubble is curious,' the Mouse said. 'I've seen bubbles like that in other levels.'

'I think all the bubbles in levels are low in the middle because they are all affected by gravity!'

The Wise Old Owl swoops down from a tree, pats the Mouse on the back, shakes her head in disgust at the Squirrel, and glares at the old Coyote.

'The readings of the carpenter's level here and around the world show two things,' Owl said. 'One, that small flat areas can be found anywhere on Earth, and two, that the bubble in the carpenter's level in every location bends downward in the middle due to gravity. It proves the exact opposite of a flat Earth.'

47

'It proves that every reading shows that the Earth is a sphere with a gravitational pull to the center of the Earth.' Owl said. 'Just like the level of water in a glass is not exactly level. The water level is higher on the sides due to capillary tension and lower in the middle of the water column due to gravity that evens out. In weightless space, a carpenter's level would be useless because the bubble inside the level's vial would float freely.'

The Coyote turned angry. 'I don't believe you,' he said as he stomped away.

The Mouse supports the Owl. 'Facts are true whether you believe them or not.'

'Admit it, Coyote,' the Squirrel said. 'The Earth is a sphere like all the other planets!'

Discussion Questions:
Was the Coyote guilty of confirmation bias, bad science, or both?
Was he pretending to practice science?
Was the carpenter's level the right tool to use?

Supporting Information: There is a long list of supporting evidence to prove the Coyote wrong, whereas he would find little to prove the Earth is flat. Ancient Indian texts like the Rigveda (~1500 BCE) described the Earth as spherical. Later texts, including works by Aryabhata (476–550 CE), explicitly stated that the Earth is a rotating sphere. Early observations by Pythagoras (~500 BCE) and Aristotle (~350 BCE) indicated the Earth was a sphere. Eratosthenes (~240 BCE), a Greek mathematician, used observations of the Sun's angle at two locations (Alexandria and Syene) to calculate the Earth's circumference with surprising accuracy. During the Age of Exploration (15th-16th centuries), the spherical Earth was widely accepted among educated Europeans, and Polynesian, Chinese, and Viking mariners used the curvature of the Earth for navigation long before Columbus's voyages. Some Native American cultures had a profound understanding of astronomy and navigation. Though less documented, these observations likely contributed to an implicit recognition of the Earth's curvature. Airplane pilots and Astronauts in space confirmed that the Earth is a sphere!

Beware of Other Science Pretenders

Fortune Telling: Fortune tellers pretend to predict the future with tarot cards, palm readings, crystal balls, or astrology despite no scientific proof they work. Usually, people pay top dollar for vague or generalized statements that can apply to anyone.

Horoscopes and Astrology: Scientific tests have shown no connection between astrological signs and personality traits or life events. Astrology claims are not testable with science.

Homeopathy: Scientific studies consistently show no evidence that homeopathy is more effective than a placebo.

Energy Healing: There's no evidence to prove the mysterious Reiki or Crystal Healing energy fields and no physical mechanism to explain how they would work. Again, controlled studies fail to show effects beyond placebo.

Psychic Abilities: Claims to read minds, communicate with the dead, Extra Sensory Perception (ESP), or see the future have never been demonstrated under controlled conditions.

Conclusion: Buyer beware! These pretenders and practices exist because people believe what aligns with their expectations or they seek comfort, hope, or a sense of control over their future. Fortune tellers, horoscopes, and miracle cures are widely promoted, making them familiar and socially accepted without evidence. Without a strong understanding of scientific methods, people may not recognize pseudoscience. Remain skeptical and save your money and dignity.

What is a Myth-Understanding?

The old Coyote, Squirrel, and Mouse were enjoying a walk in the park when Squirrel asked Coyote for advice.

'Coyote, do you still believe Sandy Claws is real?' Squirrel said with a trembling voice.

Coyote puffed up his chest, honored to be asked such a difficult question by the young Squirrel.

'Sandy Claws – do you mean the half-cat and half-eagle who flies kitty toys to all good little kittens and cats around the world?' Coyote asked the Squirrel.

Squirrel got excited just hearing the name Sandy Claws. 'That's him!'

The Mouse shook her head, 'No' and added, 'Please tread carefully, Coyote. Squirrel is still young.'

The mean Coyote snickered at the Mouse. 'I'm smart enough to know what to say, Mouse! I was young once, too! I learned all about myths in school, including Hercules, the half-god and half-man from ancient Greece. He was the strongest human alive.'

The Coyote turns meanly to Squirrel. 'Or the half-man, half-bull, called the Minotaur, who hides underground waiting for his next meal – children sent to him as a sacrifice.'

The Squirrel's eyes open wide in fright.
The Mouse gets angry at Coyote. 'You're scaring Squirrel!'

The Coyote shrugs like he doesn't care.

The Wise Old Owl swoops down from a tree, pats the Mouse on the back, smiles compassionately at the Squirrel, and glares at the old Coyote.

'A myth is an old story made up by our ancestors to help us understand the world and our place within it,' the Wise Old Owl said to the Squirrel. 'Some myths are inspirational, like Hercules, while some myths promote good behavior, like Sandy Claws, and other myths, like the Minotaur, are meant to scare us into being good.'

'Like Darth Vader?' asked Squirrel.

'I suppose so,' the Wise Old Owl said.

'Once youngsters learn to be good on their own accord, the myth is no longer necessary, except to honor the traditional storytelling. Sometimes our elders aren't as honest as they should be with grown children regarding myths, making it difficult for them to tell fact from fiction later in life. For example, the myth of Hercules, half-man and half-god, blurs what it means to be human. I learned early in life that Hercules was 'just a myth.'

Discussion question: Can you name other myths you've been told and understand why they were told to you as true stories by your elders?

Supporting Information: Myths often serve as a form of early education and religious instruction, especially in societies with limited literacy. All civilizations created myths. They are based on fictional stories that were passed down orally through generations. They are a way to make sense of the complex aspects of life through symbolic stories. Eventually, some people learn they are highly unlikely to be real, while many people struggle to admit that truth.

Limits of the Scientific Method

The scientific method is a powerful tool for exploring the natural world, but it has limits. Here are some areas or questions that cannot be directly tested using the scientific method:

- **Subjective experiences:** Personal tastes, preferences, or feelings.
- **Ethical and moral questions:** What is right or wrong? What is the "best" system of government?
- **Philosophical questions:** What is consciousness? Does "free will" exist?
- **Metaphysical or supernatural claims:** Does God (or gods) exist? Is there an afterlife?
- **Abstract or value-based questions:** What is the meaning of life? What makes art beautiful?
- **Cultural or Religious Beliefs:** Beliefs that rely on faith, not empirical evidence.

Science relies on forming hypotheses that can be observed, tested, and potentially falsified. These lack measurable outcomes or fall outside the realm of empirical investigation.

Practical Advice in Everyday Life

1. **Stay Curious:** Treat everyday situations as opportunities to learn and solve puzzles. Ask questions about things you see and hear.
2. **Document Findings:** Keep notes or mental logs of observations and results. Fact-check claims you see and hear. Remain skeptical.
3. **Embrace Trial and Error:** Mistakes are part of the process; refine your approach when needed. Become a life-long learner.
4. **Use Reliable Tools and Sources**: In research, prioritize credible sources over biased sources and hearsay.
5. **Be Open to Change:** Adjust your thinking based on evidence, even if it challenges initial assumptions. [This is the most difficult challenge you'll face!]
6. **Start Small:** Practice with simple, everyday problems to build a habit of sharp thinking.

Additional Resources

These are my two favorite books about sharper thinking. Many more books and peer-reviewed scientific journal articles would do equally well.

1. "How to Think About Weird Things: Critical Thinking for a New Age" by Lewis Vaughn and Theodore Schick (2023) McGraw Hill.
2. "The Demon-Haunted World: Science as a Candle in the Dark" (1997) by Carl Sagan and Ann Druyan. Ballantine Books.

About the Author

Tom Stohlgren was born in Oakland, California. He holds a Ph.D. from the University of California, Davis. He enjoyed long careers as a Research Scientist for the U.S. Department of the Interior (1977-2018) and a Senior Research Scientist for Colorado State University (1991-2020), where he conducted ecological research, taught classes, and advised graduate students. He published over 210 scientific papers and one textbook. He enjoyed teaching classes in ecology, modeling species invasions, statistics, and especially, critical thinking. He's been happily married for over 43 years, has three grown children, and wears Hawaiian shirts every day. He treats every day like a toy.

Acknowledgments: He thanks Dan Binkley, Jim and Linda Detling, Vinceena Irgens, Sunil Kumar, and Mike, Connor, and Michelle Stohlgren for comments and suggestions on earlier versions of the booklet.

Made in United States
Troutdale, OR
01/05/2025